Pieces of Palestine : a collection of poems

Lilufa Uddin

BookLeaf
Publishing

India | USA | UK

Presentation by *BookLeaf Publishing*

Web: www.bookleafpub.com

E-mail: info@bookleafpub.com

ISBN: 9789360940911

First edition 2024

First and foremost, I would like to dedicate this to my brothers and sisters in Palestine. My heart aches deeply for you all and yearns for your relief, safety and happiness. May Allah alleviate all of your suffering, and grant you all the most beautiful patience and strength and may you all rejoice in the highest ranks of Jannah (heaven). I hope these poems illustrate your inspiring faith in such turbulent times of great adversity. I hope you know that you are all the soul of my soul and I admire you with all my soul.

Secondly, I would like to dedicate this to the Muslim ummah - I hope the poems resonate with you and allow you to empathise with our brothers and sisters in Palestine. I hope each poem impels you to show gratitude to Allah in all circumstances. As Prophet Muhammad may the blessings and peace of Allah be upon him) says in a hadith : "How wonderful the affair of the believer is! Indeed, all of his affairs are good for him. This is for no one but the believer. If something good happens to him, he is greatful to Allah, which is good for him. And if something bad happens to him, he has patience, which is good for him."

ACKNOWLEDGEMENT

I would like to first thank Allah for making this possible. Alhamdulillah (all praises and thanks belongs to Allah).

I would like to thank every Palestinian person I have been blessed to meet, who has offered me their time, kind words and encouragement. I truly appreciate you all. In addition, I would like to thank all the books I have read, that have offered me solace and company when I have been alone. Dear books, you have moulded me into the reader and writer I am today.

PREFACE

By virtue of our emaan (faith), we will not be disconnected from the pain of our brothers and sisters in Palestine. As Prophet Muhammad (may the blessings and peace of Allah be upon him) says : "Verily the believer among the people of faith is like the face of the head to the body. The believer feels pain for the people of faith, just as the body feels pain for the head." The genocide happening in Palestine is the sorrow and hardship of every believer. Firstly, they are our brothers and sisters in Islam, we are one family. Secondly, Palestinians are being massacred, violated and deprived of every basic human right. Can you imagine carrying the limbs of your child's mutilated body? How would your heart bear seeing your dead mother's body being eaten by dogs? What would you do if you had to choose between dirty water and death?

The Palestinian people are indeed special human beings, who have touched the hearts and souls of many all over the world. They are physical manifestations of courage and hope. Courage and hope in such a cowardly and cold world.

The land of Palestine is no ordinary land, it is blessed land and very sacred for Muslims. Masjid-Al-Aqsa is in Palestine and it is mentioned in the Qur'an. Historically, Masjid-Al-Aqsa was the first qibla (direction of prayer) for Muslims and it is the second oldest masjid (mosque) in the world. Moreover, it is indeed in this very masjid, that our noble prophet Muhammad (may the blessings of and peace of Allah be upon him) led all the prophets in prayer. Is it any wonder that this land is regarded so highly to the believers?

Do not weep O Abdullah!
Your brother is a martyr.
Rejoice!
Praise Allah for granting your brother such a
lofty status.
Say Alhamdulillah.

Patience is not simply the ability to wait but the
ability to keep a good attitude while waiting.

Do not weep O Abdullah!
Your brother is very special.
Smile!
Thank Allah for honouring your brother with
reward in the next life ..
The everlasting abode

Patience is not simply the ability to wait but the
ability to keep a good attitude while waiting.

Do not weep O Abdullah!
Your brother is now at peace.
Delight!
Glorify Allah for what he has decreed

For indeed Allah is the most wise and the most just.

Do not fret dear son, victory is near.
Allah upholds his promises.
As he has said to us ..
'Verily with hardship comes ease'.

Lower your head in submission to Allah, dear son.
Your reunion with your brother in Jannah will be a great one.

You and your brother Abdur Rahman are the coolness of my eyes.

Do not weep O Abdullah!
Patience is the crown the Palestinians wear!

2

Ya Abdur Rahman ..
My heart is bleeding and my eyes are stinging
with tears
You have left this world and taken the sun with
you.
In my heart, sadness dances with my yearning
for your joyful company.

Breakfast is not the same anymore.
I miss scooping up the fresh bread mum kneaded
in the morning into olive oil, and giving you the
first bite.
My dear sweet brother.

I miss rushing to Friday prayer with you by my
side.
We would stand side by side, shoulder to
shoulder.
We would race to make it to the first row.
How proud you have made me to call you my
brother.
You were a righteous young man,who many
took inspiration from.

The children in the village sing your praises.

They say you are a top footballer and that they
want to play another game with you.
The widows say that nobody has your charm.
They say you were like a son to them.

I wake up in the middle of the night and make
du'a to be reunited with you.
You cherished making the orphans smile.
So now I give them dates to eat, as charity in
your name.

I see your name in the sky
I hear your laugh when I'm standing on the roof.

My chest tightens and my heart hurts me deeply.

My dearest sweetest brother, tell me, where do I
find a brother like you?

3

Sweeter than honey..
Your smiles would cure every ache in my body
and sorrow in my heart.

I have died a million times over and over again.
What am I now?
Just a lifeless woman, walking around with an
empty soul inside.

My arms extend, hoping to reach your beautiful
faces - but you are deep into the Earth's soil..
and so only emptiness reaches my arms.

Even the oxygen I breathe in seems to suffocate
me with pain.

Sanad you used to hold my hand and tell me
every morning, that I will forever be Queen of
the family.

Bisan my darling daughter, you took such care
of oiling my hair every night. Who will care to
care after my hair with such love again?

My hope was to protect you both until you reach old age.

How was I to know you will leave this world before me?

My worst nightmare has come true.

In Allah we trust.

Just as Musa's mother did before us.

We trust in Allah.

Allah is great and he is the most generous!

4

The world indulges in eating and savouring the
finest of foods ..
Whilst we celebrate the hunting of a donkey for
dinner.

Oh how times have changed.
For the worse.
Indeed, there was time in which Palestinians
raised their own livestock and cooked the best
meat and chicken.

100 days without rice, bread or chicken.
We stare at the dead humans and animals
scattered on our streets and suddenly our
appetites disappear again.

Aid trucks? What aid trucks?
Evil oppressors bid farwell to numerous aid
trucks.
But whoever relies on other people's supplies,
will find his hunger lasts longer

And so we learn to accept the donkey.
Never have Palestinians wondered about eating
donkey for dinner.

But oh how times have changed.

Yes, carry on sitting on your thrones.
Why move?
You are comfortable right?
We are uncomfortable, no?
We cause you discomfort, yes?

Me and my people, we sit on the floor.
Rationing pigeon meet amongst the families in
the village ..
We are one
and you are all one
We pray for our survival.

A light belly and heavy heart is what we carry.

5

Mint leaves are my favourite.
How gloriously green they are..
and oooof their aroma ..mmm .. tantalising.

I used to buy mint leaves for my mother every
morning from Abu Salman.
Now, Abu Salman is dead and he has taken the
mint leaves with him.

Me and my friend Hamza put pretty flowers in
our tea now.
Our favourite coffeeshop has been shattered into
a million pieces.
We sit on rocks, and look happily at the rubble
around us.
What a delightful image. How artistic. How
profound.

Even a little evil is too much evil.
Please remember that!

Hamza and I inhale the musk emanating from
the bodies of our people around us. For this
smell of musk is better than all the expensive
perfumes the rest of the world wear.

Always laugh when you can.
It is cheap medicine.

6

My name is Suqaar.
Mama used to say, that whenever I am around,
nobody needs sugar in their tea.
My mother would boast that I am sweeter than
my name.
She is the only woman that would make me
blush.

My mum called me Suqaar.
I also called her Suqaar.
I am her youngest child and only child alive.

I had four brothers and two sisters.
Ali, Uthman, Umar, Bilal, Amina and Halima.

And my father?
Oh they killed him too.

I miss my father. His name is Waleed.
Bold.
Intelligent.
Brave.
Amazing.
Generous.

Baba, you used to get jealous of me calling
Mama Suqaar.
So I used to call you Jawharaat Al Aba (Gem of
fatherhood)
Baba thank you for your sacrifices.
You payed for my education.
I am educated.
You taught me how to life weights.
I am strong
You never left my side.
I am heartbroken Baba

I could never be a quarter of the man he was.

He risked his life as a journalist to show the
world the truth.

And yet, still so many remain silent and
indifferent.

All I have left in this world, is Mama Suqaar.

Oh world, oh privileged world ..

Please help me save the sweetest thing to me.

Mama

7

'How deep can a heart sink?', I ask myself ..

Light is absent in the cell that I have been
residing in.

Scars on my back, compete with each other
with who can cause me the most burning
sensation.

Bruises on my face reassure one another that I
am still handsome, no matter how many punches
and kicks my face takes.

A constant piercing noise in my ears ..
Mouth as dry as the desert,
I rummage in the dark for something to clean my
teeth with.
I pick up a plank of wood, and snap it into
smaller pieces and use it to brush my teeth.
Blood starts pouring at my mouth and I vomit at
the same time.

My head starts spinning and I start getting the
flashbacks.
Hot boiling water poured all over my body,

Kicked in my stomach by soldiers demanding
for me to denounce my faith ..
Rats being thrown into my cell along with dead
bodies..

Oceans of sorrow move within me.

I use my broken arm to stroke my other arm, as I
long for care and affection.
I reminisce on my mother's touch and love, and
how she would sacrifice her health and sleep just
to stay by my side whenever I was in pain.

Now I am motherless. In a inhumane dungeon of
a cell, struggling to breathe and striving to recite
the verses from the Qur'aan I have memorised.

Everytime the soldiers hear me reciting Qur'aan,
they stamp on my face and spit at me.

I use my broken arm to stroke my other arm,
longing for affection and love from another
human.

7 months and 22 days I have been abused and
tortured in this place ..

Tears fill my tired eyes, hoping to reach my
mother's heart.

I just want someone to care for me. Someone to
hold my hand .
I have nobody.
I taste my own tears, as they trickle down my
face.
Bitter, salty and a little sweet.
Sweet.. how you wonder? My tears were the
first bit of water my innocent mouth had tasted
in days.
As I tried to keep my tears in my mouth as long
as I could ..
A solider rushes in positioning a rifle gun to my
eyes
'Do you see now, that we are more superior to
you?' he roars

Silence.

My eyes confront his eyes and there lays the
answer to his dishonourable question.

8

Skipping down the road with my sister Reem,
we were so excited to be going to school.

Mama had packed us Knafeh into our
schoolbags.

I pretended not to hear the bombs above us. I
looked at my sister Reem.
She was also pretending not to hear the bombs.

They call us the lionesses of Khan Younis. They
say we are from a family of lions.
Baba was the biggest lion of us all. Our
protector, but he is no longer here.

We run down an alleway, taking a shortcut to
school.

All the uncles in the market greet us warmly.
The wonderful aroma of fresh bread, cheese,
olive oil and herbs and spices enters my nose
and makes me smile.

Uncle Rashid shoves some pomegranate juice in
mine and Reem's hands.

"With health and comfort my darling daughters"
he says.
"Shukran uncle", we say in unison.
 I give him a hug, pull his beard jokingly and run
away with my sister towards our school.

My hands begin to shake.

"I miss Baba", I say to Reem, my juice spilling
over me.

Reem embraces me and strokes my hair.
"In Jannah, hayati, in Jannah."

I hug Reem tight and she walks me to my
classroom.

"Ustada!" I scream.

My teacher lays dead on the floor, blood gushing
down her face.
The soldiers surround her and start firing at
students.

I look down at my hands.

Is this the fate that my mother carried me nine
long hard months for?

9

How wealthy am I?
I am cycling, carrying my son's mutilated arms,
legs and hands.
How privileged am I?
To carry my son by myself to the grave.
How blessed am I?
That my son died a martyr.

Sufficient for us is Allah and he is the best
disposer of affairs.

Musa was the last family member I had left.
His mother and sisters were killed by an
airstrike, on their way to Rafah.

Musa was my best friend.

Musa would recite verses of the Qur'aan he had
learnt and memorised.
I would correct him and celebrate his
achievements.
He loved football and so a day did not go by,
that we did not play football together.
He thought he was a better football player than
me. Hmm.

Musa and I would pray together on the street and gather the local men to offer prayers.

I have lost count of how many times we would offer the funeral prayer in a week.

These days the bodies are being eaten by stray animals that have escaped the zoo.

Lions and dogs alike, eat away the hearts of our mothers, fathers, children, brothers and sisters.

My Musa.

I just want to hear him call me Baba one more time.

Musa. My heart's heart.

10

We are from the blessed and sacred land of
where our prophets were born,
In Masjid Al Aqsa, is where our prophets
prayed!
What a honourable beautiful place, we reside in.
Even if the world's corrupt leaders offered me all
the world's money and treasures,
Never would I disobey Allah's commands
Never would I turn my back on my land or my
country.

So do as you please.
Take away our people, our animals and our olive
trees.

We will live on and victory will prevail for the
believers.

11

Umm Rayhaan is the kindest and most loving aunty in the neighbourhood.

Mama and Baba are no more.

My little sister was kidnapped 17 days ago and I have no idea where she is.

Umm Rayhaan said she has gained another son through me.

Friday, the best day of the week has come.

Aunty said "I will take you to the market and buy you the best meat from the market after Friday prayer."

And indeed she honoured her promise.

She sat outside her tent and lit up a fire.

Love is a need of every human to survive and thrive.

My parents were martyred whilst they were
doing their ablution for the afternoon prayer.

The house my dad had worked so hard to build,
was destroyed in seconds.

When I had heard my parents had died, my body
shivered aggressively.

I felt like the blood in my body had stopped
flowing.

My soul ached so badly and my heart competed
with my soul, in keeping me going ..

For, mentally I was dead. My whole life
revolved around Mama and Baba.

A 30 year old man, but to them, I will always be
their baby.

Mama and Baba disappeared with all the colour
in the world.

Now all I see is grey rubble around me.

Umm Rayhaan poured water on a heart, which
was slowly burning to death.

They say it takes a village to raise a child.

I am no longer a child, but I yearn the love. The love of my people.

Where are they?

Deep down below, they are buried.

Some .. their body parts scattered on the streets.

I look up at aunty Umm Rayhaan and my eyes well up with tears.

She scoops up some meat and bread and puts it into my mouth.

"I am your mama, until you are reunited with your mama in Jannah."

12

"Chocolate biscuit, Baba. Chocolate Biscuit Baba!"

"Baba. Baba. Baba."

Zakariyaa's voice is imprinted on my mind.

I hear his voice everywhere I walk and everywhere I sit.

All my precious boy had asked me for was a chocolate biscuit.

He had humbly accepted me and his mother feeding him grass, just to survive.

I feel shy and dissapppointed I could not provide better for my diamond son.

What was I to do?

Bakeries had been bombed.

Electricity had been cut.

No water.

Zakariyaa only asked me for a chocolate biscuit.

I took my last money to fulfil my son's wish.

I ran excitedly back to the house to put a smile
on my son's face,

That opportunity ceased to exist. My son was
gone.

Brutally murdered.

I clung to Zakariyaa's neck and kissed my son on
the forehead.

Mountains came crushing down on my heart.

I looked to the sky and proclaimed "Sufficient
for us is Allah and he is the best disposer of
affairs."

Kissing Zakariyaa's hand, I placed the chocolate
biscuits in his right hand.
"Baba, eat these in Jannah. May you be granted
everything your beautiful heart desires and more
in Jannah. Ameen."

13

Sparkling humbly with such beauty, the
shimmery blue sea lays still.
My mind is deeply at unrest and my heart is
becoming weaker by the day.

I came by the sea, to taste a moment of
tranquillity.
How generous of a friend is the sea, for the calm
and serenity it offers me.
I wish I could keep this friend with me always,
but I have been denied this meeting with my
friend for weeks.

I have been running around from place to place
fleeing for my safety.

But there is no place in Palestine that is safe.

The evil monsters have destroyed our houses,
our shops, our streets and most importantly
human life.

Water has been scarce for days, due to the heavy
bombardment ..

and so I leap into the sea and my eyes start to
weep ...

my tears merge with the water in the sea.

I couldn't even wash the body of my beloved
father for his funeral.

That regret will forever stay with me, though it
was beyond my control.

I did not know he was killed and had found out
from neighbours.

Guilt started to bother me, so I ran out of the sea
and ambled onto the beach ..

I looked around me ..

I saw so many children rolling around on the
sand and teasing each other, playing games,
laughing and smiling.

My people are great.
My people are strong.
My people are great.

14

Knock our houses down, we will lay on the
streets
Kill our children, we will bury them with
honour.
Keep food and water away from us, we will still
stand tall, with our heads held high.

For what is this life, but a number of days?

And what is happiness, but a fleeting emotion?

The bombs in the sky visit us more than
happiness does, and yet we smile.

Why do we still smile?

Because indeed our Lord's promises are true.

And on that great day, when people will see the
reward for those that were tested in this world -
they will have wished they endured what we did
and more.

We are the winners.
We have been honoured.

We have been blessed.

So, do not feel sorry for us.

Honour can never be taken from the blessed
land.

Victory is near and Allah's help will surely
come.

So we remain patient, for Allah is with the
patient.

Patience is beautiful.

15

O Baba, your heart is bigger than the world and
all that it contains ..
You buried eight of your children, 48 of your
grandchildren ..
all as martyrs.
Millions of times your heart broke.
But never did you utter a word of disgrace.
Never did you frown.
You always glorified Allah, in every
circumstance.

I look at you with the deepest and fondest
admiration.
Never have you missed a single prayer.
Everyday you offer charity to someone
Be it even a date split in half.

Half of your face is burnt from trying to save me
from a burning school.
You are a hero Baba. My hero.
You only have one eye.
I wish I could give you one of my eyes.
But ..
my eyes are not as beautiful as your lovely green
eyes!

Baba, thank you
Thank you for setting such a high standard for
me.
Thank you for all the sleepless nights you
endured ..
To keep watch over us, as drones and bombs
decorated our night skies.

16

Uncle Wasim and Aunty Amira had invited us for lunch.
They had cooked Makloubeh.
My favourite.
Aunty Amira made us this amazing refreshing drink too.
Jallab.
MMM. YUM!

I dip my finger in the drink .. is this real?
My stomach sang a song of thanks to me.
My soul was enriched.

For over 134 days, me and my siblings were eating left overs from our neighbours. Some days we did not eat at all.
Mama would cry and wipe her tears away and she would sit us down and remind us that Jannah awaits, and the greatest feast awaits.

Baba could not bear to see us straving. So he would walk off and cry secretly.

Today, we sit at Uncle Wasim's and Aunty
Amira's house with gratitude.

BANG! The door opens and the soldiers push
Mama and Aunty Amira to one corner.

"You filthy aminals!" they shout at us all.

Baba and Uncle Wasim get up, but the soldiers
shoot them in their faces.

They drop to the ground like flies.

Two lions leave us.

Traumatised ...

Heart .. broken ... Heart .. gone..

Soul ... shattered ... soul ..

They took Mama and Aunty Amira away,
beating them with the ends of their guns.

My fingers felt like they would fall off from
shaking.

Is this the price for loving to eat Makloubeh?

17

Humiliation is the new honour.

Hands tied behind our backs, me and the men
from my village are demanded to sit on the floor
and chant a song in Hebrew.

We refuse.

Instead, we sing in Arabic.

Oh how beautiful Arabic is, its sweet melody, its
sophisticated vastness, is the reason for its
strength and persevation.

Oh sweet Arabic. You soothe souls that do not
understand your meaning.

Our resistance leads us to being thrown into a
ditch and covered in dirt.

Today, it is us.

Tomorrow the dirt they throw over us, will be
the same dirt over them.

18

That's my MAMA! Noooooooooooooooooooooo!

MAMA!

Ya MAMA!

Please please do not leave me alone in this
world!

MAMA!

I run with the doctors running with the hospital
bed with my mum laying down.

So weak and damaged.

Her brain is about to fall off her head and her
legs have been amputated.

Oh world, do you like to see this?

Oh world, do you not have mothers too?

Oh world, are my screams .. music to your ears?

A doctor tells me that this is not my mother.
He whispers to another doctor, that they cannot
save my mother and in moments she will die.

Fierce and persistent, I tell them I know it is my
mother.

I push them away and I hold my mother's hands.
They are covered in rice.

Does your mother like rice?

My mother could not even finish the meal she
had taken so long to prepare.

She will never see me get married, or meet my
future children.

She will never get to see the beautiful moon in
the amazing night sky.

But, she is now at peace.

Away from the constant ambulance sirens,
screams of children under rubble and the
continous air strikes killing our people.

Mama I love you.

19

I wish the camels from Saudi would visit us.

My legs are tired and my head hurts.

The Palestinians have been riding me to get to
their hospitals, as electricity has been cut and
fuel is not available.

Horse I am, but I too have emotions.

Devastated and defated, I feel.

I am carrying people who no longer call me by
name.

They just tell me to go faster.
They cry and they shout.

Their sad faces bring tears to my eyes.

I walk along a shattered city that no longer has
people or olive trees.

The only thing that brings comfort to my heart is
hearing the call to prayer and wtinessing the

believers hasten to pray, even in the midst of
agony and pain.

I love you oh Palestinians.

I do not want to see your tears anymore.

I want you to hear you call my name again.

I wish the Camels from Arabia would visit us.

I need a break too.

20

Hopping from tent to tent ..
I take a sweet to each child and tell them they
are special.
Chosen.
Blessed and honoured.

The rainwater has flooded the inside of the tents.

The elderly use rocks as pillows and pieces of
cardboard as blankets.

Children raise their hands and pray for
sustenance and safety.

Mothers cry audibly but silent tears too.

Fathers, grief-stricken, look lost and shaken.

Reminders benefit the believers.

And so I remind my people of the great rewards
in Jannah that await us.

They take comfort in what I say and say words
of prayer for me.

I place my head on the floor and prostrate to
Allah.

Thank you Allah, for preserving me.

21

O precious children of Palestine,

With your angelic smiles and adorable eyes,

Do not fret, and do not despair.

For you are the kings and queens of this world
that we take inspiration from.

Continue to shame us and motivate us with your
faith and manners.

Look at the stars and count yourselves at the best
of them.

Take every flower from the ground that you see
and know that the beauty of nature forever will
be.

Pray to Allah. He is the All-Seeing and
All-Hearing.

As Allah says, " Do not think 'O Prophet' that
Allah is unaware of what the wrongdoers do. He

only delays them until a day when their eyes will stare in horror."

Recite the Qur'aan and remain strong and steadfast as you are.

We are rooting for you, oh children of Palestine.

www.ingramcontent.com/pod-product-compliance
Lightning Source LLC
LaVergne TN
LVHW021303200726
843509LV00012B/1765